Imagine this:

One day
while walking in the woods,
you spot a towering tree
with a hole big enough
to slip inside.

So you do.

As you crouch down
and close your eyes,
the sounds of the outside world
fade away.
And you wonder . . .

What would it be like
to live inside a tree?

For my parents,
who encouraged
me to be curious
—M.S.

To Kirsten
—A.H.

The artist used acrylic
paint and charcoal pencil on
various types of wood and
digital collage to create the
illustrations for this book.

TREE
HOLE
HOMES

DAYTIME DENS AND NIGHTTIME NOOKS

MELISSA STEWART
& AMY HEVRON

RANDOM HOUSE STUDIO
NEW YORK

A tree hole home
can be big or small,

In March, a female barred owl looks for a large tree hole with a wide opening. It's the perfect place to raise a trio of fuzzy owlets.

A deer mouse prefers a safe, snug spot. It chooses a tree hole high off the ground with a 1 inch (2.5 cm) opening.

calm and quiet,

A fisher spends most of its life alone. Its carefully chosen tree hole is a retreat for sleeping, staying warm in chilly weather, and eating prey in peace.

or bursting with life.

In early summer, a female raccoon moves into a tree hole 10 to 40 feet (3 to 12 m) off the ground. A few days later, she gives birth to as many as seven cubs.

The little ones eat and grow, wrestle and play inside their busy home. After two months, the cubs begin to explore the world outside their tree.

A tree hole home can be
deep in the woods

High in the rain forest canopy, a female tree frog searches for a tree hole filled with rainwater. She attaches her eggs to the walls above the pool.

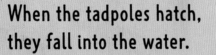

When the tadpoles hatch, they fall into the water.

Every few days, the female frog returns to the sky-high nest. She checks on the tadpoles and lays unfertilized eggs for them to eat.

or at the edge of a field,

Eastern bluebirds choose
tree holes that look out over
open fields. To make a nest,
the female weaves together
grass and pine needles. She
may add soft feathers on top
before laying up to seven
pale blue eggs.

built by a bird

Male and female black-capped chickadees work together to hollow out a home in the soft wood of a dead tree. The little birds can live in trees that are just 4 inches (10 cm) across.

Western gray squirrels
often choose tree holes
built by woodpeckers.
These homes have a
smooth circular opening.

or created by nature.

A lightning strike can split a tree open, forming the perfect sleeping spot for a colony of little brown bats.

When the wind blows a branch off a tree, a thick lip forms around the wound. Over time, insects, fungi, and bacteria eat away at the wood. Eventually, they may create a hollow big enough to house a bobcat family.

During the day, a Liberian tree hole crab rests inside a wet hollow 3 to 6 feet (1 to 2 m) off the ground. At night, it skitters to the forest floor and hunts for small insects.

A tree hole home can be a daytime den

or a nighttime nook,

A black spiny-tailed iguana
spends its days dining on
leaves and fruit. At night,
it sleeps in a tree hole. If
a hungry boa constrictor
slithers by, the lizard uses
its spiky tail to block the
opening of its home.

a springtime refuge,

In spring, a female wood duck lays up to sixteen eggs inside a tree hole. For the next month, the cavity hides the eggs and the female from predators.

A day after the ducklings hatch,
they jump out of the hole and . . .

SPLASH!

They land safely in the
water below.

an autumn invitation,

Each autumn, an American black bear searches for a snug spot to spend the winter. It may squeeze into a tree hole up to 60 feet (18 m) above the ground.

or even a year-round haven.

After a night of cruising through the forest, sugar gliders return to their tree hole home. Sleeping in a huddled heap keeps the little marsupials warm and cozy all year long.

**A tree hole home
is the perfect place**
for nesting and resting.

It's a safe, cozy spot

to escape from the outside world.

MORE ABOUT TREE HOLE DWELLERS

BARRED OWLS

Scientific name: *Strix varia*
Size: 17–20 inches (43–50 cm)
Habitat: Forest, open woodlands
Range: East, Midwest, and Pacific Northwest North America
Diet: Squirrels, chipmunks, mice, voles, rabbits, birds, frogs, salamanders
Life span: 18 years
Fun fact: A barred owl's call sounds like it's hooting, "Who-cooks-for-you, who-cooks-for-you-all?"

DEER MOUSE

Scientific name: *Peromyscus maniculatus*
Size: 3–4 inches (8–10 cm)
Habitat: Woodlands, grasslands, deserts
Range: North America, except southeastern United States
Diet: Insects, seeds, fruits, fungi, nuts
Life span: About 1 year
Fun fact: Sometimes a deer mouse eats its droppings. It might seem like a nasty habit, but it helps the mini-mammal get all the nutrients it needs to live and grow.

FISHER

Scientific name: *Martes pennanti*
Size: 30–47 inches (90–120 cm)
Habitat: Forests
Range: Northern United States, Canada
Diet: Snowshoe hares, porcupines, squirrels, mice, birds
Life span: Up to 10 years
Fun fact: When a fisher runs, it holds its tail high above the ground, like a house cat.

RACCOON

Scientific name: *Procyon lotor*
Size: 16–28 inches (40–70 cm)
Habitat: Forests, wetlands, urban areas
Range: Throughout North America
Diet: Insects, worms, crayfish, fish, frogs, bird eggs, fruits, nuts
Life span: Up to 3 years
Fun fact: Raccoons use more than 50 different sounds to communicate with one another.

TREE FROG

Scientific name: *Frankixalus jerdonii*
Size: 1.7 inches (4.3 cm)
Habitat: Rain forests
Range: Northeastern India
Diet: Plants
Life span: Unknown
Fun fact: Scientists thought this frog was extinct until they rediscovered it in 2007.

EASTERN BLUEBIRD

Scientific name: *Sialia sialis*
Size: 7 inches (17.5 cm)
Habitat: Open woodlands, fields
Range: Eastern United States, central Mexico, southeastern Canada
Diet: Insects, fruit
Life span: 6–10 years
Fun fact: Bluebird chicks stay in their nest for 15 to 20 days after hatching. During that time, their parents carry away the chicks' fecal sacs to keep the nest clean and odor free.

BLACK-CAPPED CHICKADEE

Scientific name: *Poecile atricapillus*
Size: 4–6 inches (10–15 cm)
Habitat: Forests
Range: Northern United States, Canada
Diet: Insects, seeds, berries
Life span: 2–3 years
Fun fact: A chickadee is named after its *chick-a-dee-dee!* warning call. When the little bird is extremely worried or upset, it adds extra "dees" to the end of the call.

WESTERN GRAY SQUIRRELS

Scientific name: *Sciurus griseus*
Size: 18–24 inches (45–60 cm)
Habitat: Forests
Range: Pacific Northwest of United States
Diet: Pinecone seeds, nuts, berries, fungi, bark
Life span: 7–8 years
Fun fact: A gray squirrel uses its bushy tail like a blanket in the winter and as shade from the sun in summer.

LITTLE BROWN BATS

Scientific name: *Myotis lucifugus*
Size: 3–3.5 inches (7.6–9 cm)
Habitat: Caves, forests, buildings
Range: Eastern and western United States, Canada, central Mexico
Diet: Insects
Life span: Up to 30 years
Fun fact: A little brown bat sleeps for 20 hours a day.

BOBCATS

Scientific name: *Lynx rufus*
Size: 30–40 inches (76–101 cm)
Habitat: Forests, mountains, scrublands, semi-deserts
Range: Most of United States, southern Canada, northern Mexico
Diet: Rabbits, wood rats, squirrels, birds, fish
Life span: Up to 12 years
Fun fact: A bobcat can run 30 miles (48 km) per hour and leap 10 feet (3 m) to catch prey.

LIBERIAN TREE HOLE CRAB

Scientific name: *Globonautes macropus*
Size: 1 inch (2.5 cm)
Habitat: Rain forests
Range: Western Africa
Diet: Insects
Life span: Unknown
Fun fact: Liberian tree hole crabs are in danger of going extinct. There may be as few as 2,500 alive today.

BLACK SPINY-TAILED IGUANA

Scientific name: *Ctenosaura similis*
Size: 3–4 feet (0.9–1.2 m)
Habitat: Forests, grasslands
Range: Mexico, Central America
Diet: Flowers, leaves, stems, fruit, some small animals
Life span: 15–25 years
Fun fact: The black spiny-tailed iguana is the fastest lizard on Earth. It can run 21 miles (34 km) per hour.

WOOD DUCKS

Scientific name: *Aix sponsa*
Size: 19 inches (48 cm)
Habitat: Swamps, rivers, ponds, lakes
Range: East, Northwest, and West Coast United States, southern Canada, northeastern and northwestern Mexico
Diet: Seeds, fruits, insects
Life span: 3–4 years
Fun fact: A wood duck has sharp claws that let it perch in trees.

AMERICAN BLACK BEAR

Scientific name: *Ursus americanus*
Size: 4–6 feet (1.2–1.8 m)
Habitat: Forests
Range: Northeast, Midwest, and West Coast United States, Canada
Diet: Fruits, nuts, tree buds, honey, insects, fish, dead animals
Life span: Up to 30 years
Fun fact: An American black bear can lose more than 100 pounds (45 kg) during the winter.

SUGAR GLIDERS

Scientific name: *Petaurus breviceps*
Size: 6–8 inches (15–20 cm)
Habitat: Forests
Range: Eastern Australia, Tasmania, New Guinea
Diet: Insects, tree sap
Life span: Up to 9 years
Fun fact: A sugar glider can leap the length of four school buses.

SELECTED SOURCES

Biju, S. D., et al. "*Frankixalus*, a New Rhacophorid Genus of Tree Hole Breeding Frogs with Oophagous Tadpoles." *PLOS One*, January 20, 2016.
    doi.org/10.1371/journal.pone.0145727

"Cavity Trees Are Refuges for Wildlife." Landowner Resource Centre, 2011. lrconline.com/Extension_Notes_English/pdf/cvtytrs.pdf

Coe, Fran Cafferata. "Cavity-Nesting Birds and Small Woodlands." Woodland Fish & Wildlife Group. Western Forestry and Conservation Association,
    July 2014. woodlandfishandwildlife.com/wp-content/uploads/2019/12/Cavity-Nesting-Birds-and-Small-Woodlands_reduced.pdf

The Cornell Lab of Ornithology All About Birds. allaboutbirds.org

*Elder, Scott. "Mistaken Identity." *National Geographic Kids*, April 2016, pp. 18–21.

Faccio, Steve D. "Tree Cavities: Whose Hole Is That?" *Northern Woodlands*, December 5, 2011.
    northernwoodlands.org/outside_story/article/tree-cavities-whose-hole-is-that

Hassinger, Jerry, and Jack Payne. "Dead Wood for Life." PennState Extension. College of Agricultural Science, Pennsylvania State University,
    February 15, 2005. extension.psu.edu/dead-wood-for-wildlife

*Kwok, Roberta. "As Trees Come Down, Some Hidden Homes Are Disappearing." *Science News for Students*, September 7, 2017.
    sciencenewsforstudents.org/article/trees-come-down-some-hidden-homes-are-disappearing

Newman, Doug. "Cavity Creatures." *Missouri Conservationist*. Missouri Department of Conservation, October 28, 2010.
    mdc.mo.gov/magazines/conservationist/1998-04/cavity-creatures

"Pictorial Guide of Important Fisher Habitat Structures in British Columbia." Fisher Habitat Working Group.
    bcfisherhabitat.ca/wp-content/uploads/2017/02/fisher-habitat-photo-guide-20170210.pdf

Stewart, Melissa. Personal observations recorded in nature and travel journals, 1989–present.

University of Michigan Museum of Zoology's Animal Diversity Web. animaldiversity.org

*Recommended for curious kids

FOR MORE INFORMATION ABOUT ANIMAL HOMES

Aston, Dianna Hutts. *A Nest Is Noisy*. San Francisco: Chronicle, 2015.

Bové, Jennifer. *Animal Homes*. Guilford, CT: Muddy Boots, 2016.

Evans, Shira. *Animal Homes*. Washington, DC: National Geographic Kids, 2018.

Hurley, Jorey. *Nest*. New York: Little Simon, 2015.

Packham, Chris. *Amazing Animal Homes*. New York: Sterling, 2018.

Ward, Jennifer. *Mama Built a Little Den*. San Diego: Beach Lane, 2018.

Ward, Jennifer. *Mama Dug a Little Nest*. San Diego: Beach Lane, 2014.

Wilkes, Angela. *Discover Science: Animal Homes*. New York: Kingfisher, 2017.

Text copyright © 2022 by Melissa Stewart • Jacket art and interior illustrations copyright © 2022 by Amy Hevron • All rights reserved. Published in the United States by Random House Studio, an imprint of Random House Children's Books, a division of Penguin Random House LLC, New York. • Random House Studio with colophon is a registered trademark of Penguin Random House LLC • Visit us on the Web! rhcbooks.com • Educators and librarians, for a variety of teaching tools, visit us at RHTeachersLibrarians.com

Library of Congress Cataloging-in-Publication Data

Names: Stewart, Melissa, author. | Hevron, Amy, illustrator. | Title: Tree hole homes : daytime dens and nighttime nooks / Melissa Stewart, Amy Hevron. Description: First edition. New York : Random House, [2022] | Includes bibliographical references. | Audience: Ages 4–8 | Audience: Grades 2–3 | Summary: "A playful and informative nonfiction picture book about different tree holes and the amazing animals that inhabit them" —Provided by publisher. | Identifiers: LCCN 2021047887 (print) | LCCN 2021047888 (ebook) | ISBN 978-0-593-37330-9 (hardcover) | ISBN 978-0-593-37331-6 (lib.bdg.) | ISBN 978-0-593-37332-3 (ebook) | Subjects: LCSH: Animals—Habitations—Juvenile literature. Animal-plant relationships—Juvenile literature. | Tree cavities—Juvenile literature. | Classification: LCC QL756.S846 2022 (print) | LCC QL756 (ebook) | DDC 591.56/4—dc23/eng/20211029

The text of this book is set in 39- and 17-point Argone LC Regular. • Interior design by Rachael Cole
The illustrations in this book were rendered in acrylic and marker on wood, collaged digitally.
MANUFACTURED IN CHINA • 10 9 8 7 6 5 4 3 2 1 • First Edition